Purposeful Branding:

Discovering how your gifts can help you
get unstuck in your career and best serve others

by Lori Bumgarner Béen, M.Ed.

Purposeful Branding

Copyright ©2024, by Lori Bumgarner Béen, owner of paNASH Style LLC, www.yourpassioninlife.com.

Print ISBN: 9798327502932

Cover design by author (via Canva)
Author photo by Maria Gloer Photography

Imprint: paNASH Style LLC

This publication is designed to provide competent and reliable information regarding the subject matter covered. The author specifically disclaims any liability that is incurred from the use or application of the contents of this book.

All rights reserved. No part of this book may be reproduced or transmitted in any form or by any means, electronic or mechanical, including photocopying, recording or by any information storage and retrieval systems, without the written permission from the author, except for the inclusion of brief quotations in a review.

"I was at a point where I was not sure what I wanted to do next in my career. I felt stuck. Going through the process in Lori's book helped me realize things about myself that I never would have come up with on my own. I figured out why I like doing certain things, which helped me confidently pursue and obtain a new role." Laura A., paNASH client

"Lori's book gave me the nuts and bolts of how to figure out what sets me apart from my competition so that my sales pitch is authentic and engaging. Prior to now, I was lost on how to explain my business to others. Now I have the tools to do so with clarity, authenticity, and confidence." Business owner (anonymous)

"This gives me so much relief! I'm a songwriter and, before this book, I was struggling with low self-esteem because I was always comparing myself to other songwriters. Now I know I can instead spend that time and energy embracing the things that make me different and unique from other songwriters." Deidre T., workshop participant

"This was wonderful and extremely instrumental in helping me figure out who I am. I'm now able to clearly express my vision and my mission for my career." Kaylyn S., paNASH client

TABLE OF CONTENTS

Introduction — 9

Getting Started — 19

    Your Work Is Not Your Identity

    What Makes You Unique?

    The Purpose of Purposeful Branding

    The Process of Purposeful Branding

Phase I – Preparation: Identifying and Defining Your Purposeful Brand — 35

    In Limbo and Feeling Stuck

    Exercise: Self-Examination

    Exercise: Take an Inventory

    Exercise: Fieldwork

    Exercise: Peeling the Onion

    Exercise: Knowing Your Audience

    Next Steps

Phase II – Packaging: Creating and Building Your
Purposeful Brand 61

    Coming Out of Limbo

    What's Your Message? (Vision Statement, Mission Statement, and Unique Selling Point)

    Exercise: Drafting Your Message

    Don't Forget About Your Goals

    Back It Up

    Additional Packaging Steps

Phase III – Presentation: Articulating and Enhancing Your
Purposeful Brand 81

    Building Confidence

    Things to Remember

Conclusion 91

Appendix – Recommended Resources 95

Contact Information 101

About the Author 103

INTRODUCTION

There's been a lot written on the topic of branding. This includes the book I published in 2019 entitled, *Personal Branding: Why You Need to Know What Makes You YOUnique and AWEthentic.*

When people hear the word "branding," they often think only of a company and the visual aspect of its brand, such as a company logo or the colors associated with the logo. Or they might think of the company's current slogan.

However, there is so much more to a brand. A brand encompasses a company's core values, its purpose and the reasons why the founders started the company, their goals and vision for the future of the company, and their mission and methods of carrying out their vision.

There used to be another assumption people had about brands. They thought their use was reserved only for businesses. It never occurred to most people the importance of having their own brand to guide their life's work and their career decisions.

Now, a lot of people have caught on to the importance of having a personal brand, so much so they've taken the idea of it too far and distorted it. You know what I'm talking about. What may have started out as expressing an authentic voice, quickly grew into just a lot of noise. Our Instagram feeds are now clogged with the loudness of obviously staged and posed posts by influencers trying to appear authentic. However, their priorities in their goals have shifted from solely helping others, to becoming a slave to the social media treadmill of securing more followers and more money from sponsors. Those who once were afraid as being seen as impostors have become just that.

I originally wrote the first edition of this book to introduce the idea of developing a personal brand for your career. In this newly-titled edition, I still want to teach you how branding is an important component of your career. But I also want to emphasize how to do so in a purposeful way. You were created with a set of skills, talents, abilities, passions, and experiences not to be squandered or used to serve yourself, but to serve others.

I'll show you from my own experience and the experience of my clients how important it is to have a brand that's true to your gifting and helps further your purpose (or purposes, since we often have more than just one purpose) in life for the benefit of society.

I will guide you through the steps of developing a purposeful brand guaranteed to give you confidence during your job search and throughout your career.

Of course, I'm not the first person to write or speak on the topic of branding. If you're already familiar with the concept or if you've read my previous edition of this book, you may find some of the information here to be a review. But I guarantee you'll also gain some new nuggets of knowledge and insight on the topic of purposeful branding. In fact, when I present on this topic to various groups, participants often tell me afterward they learned so many new perspectives on purposeful branding and how it differs from the noise of personal branding.

My own approach to this topic came about in a very organic (and therefore purposeful) way.

...

I've always worked as a career coach. In the beginning of my career, I served as a college career adviser. Now, I am a career coach for those who are mid-career and feel stuck in their careers. My emphasis is on helping people get unstuck and pursue their passions and purposes both in work and in life. (NOTE: this is not about following your heart irresponsibly! See my blog post entitled, "'Follow Your Heart' is Bad Advice" in the Appendix.)

But in the middle of my own career, I shifted my career coaching work to part-time while I pursued a full-time business as an image consultant, working primarily with up-and-coming recording artists in the music industry here in Nashville.

During my eight years as an image consultant, when I would first sit down with new clients, many of them couldn't answer the question, "What makes you and your music unique?" Nor could they answer, "What makes you different from all the other aspiring artists who've moved to Nashville to pursue music?"

Some didn't know the answers to those questions. Others knew the answers but couldn't articulate them.

I had to ask these questions so I could know how to build an image and brand for them that was true to both their music and their personalities. I also knew they would get this same question from potential record labels. When they couldn't answer those questions, I'd have to take a few steps back and help them either figure out their uniqueness or how to articulate it.

This happened so often it evolved into a process I now use with my career coaching clients. It's also a process I used when I was going through a transition in my own life and career, which also led to the development of my *8-Step Goal-Achievement Plan*, a supplement that works in conjunction with this purposeful branding process.

Receive the *8-Step Goal-Achievement Plan* for free when you subscribe to the paNASH newsletter at www.yourpassioninlife.com.

Of all the coaching tools I've used or developed, the Purposeful Branding program is the most popular among my clients. It serves as a foundation for all the other coaching I do with them. It helps them with everything from their resumes to job interviews and even areas of their personal lives outside of work. This program truly is the best place to start in the paNASH career coaching process.

In fact, it's been so important and foundational I was asked to present on it while on a mission trip in the jungles of the Amazon! With the help of an interpreter and translator, I used it to teach pastors from surrounding villages the importance and impact of having a vision and mission for their churches and their villages.

I wasn't quite sure how this concept would be received in such an environment. But I was pleasantly surprised at how interested the pastors were in the topic, and how much it resonated with them. This confirmed for me how this concept easily translates to various populations and different types of organizations.

It's truly amazing how God took this program all the way from Music Row in Nashville to the Amazon jungle!

And now I'm bringing it to you.

So, are you ready to find out your purposeful brand? More importantly, are you ready to find out how your brand can make a positive impact on your surrounding community and the world?

Let's get started!

GETTING STARTED

Your Work is Not Your Identity

Have you ever asked yourself, "What is my purpose in life?" It's not an uncommon question for most people. In fact, ancient philosophers spent their lives wrestling with similar questions. I've also wrestled with the same question during different life and career transitions.

The question is so broad, and it can have any number of answers, which can feel overwhelming, often resulting in discouragement. This book is not designed to answer the question, "What is my purpose in life?" for you. Instead, it provides a healthy means for helping you understand how your purpose is formed, what skills and talents you bring to the table, and what table (or tables) of people you're here to serve in the form of life, vocation, and career.

Learning to see your work as more than making a widget or making a living is part of the process outlined in this book. But it's also important to understand your work is not your identity. Thinking it is can lead to discouragement, low self-esteem, and lack of confidence, especially during the inevitable times when you, like everyone else, will experience failure in your work.

In the book, *A Matter of Dignity: Inquiries into the Humanization of Work*, author John Julian Ryan tells the story of three workers: "Three men were hard at work with sledgehammers, breaking big rocks into smaller ones. Asked what were they doing, the first answered, 'Making little rocks out of big ones.' The second replied, 'Making a living.' And the third said, 'Building a cathedral.'" Notice in the story, the third man does not say, "I am the cathedral." He said he is "building a cathedral." He is *doing* something. But this is not what gives him his identity.

What you do is not your identity. You are first and foremost a human being, not a human *doing*. Therefore, your identity comes from simply *being*, and having been made by a higher being who thought enough about you to create you. Your identity doesn't have to be proven by anything you do, especially not what you do for a living.

If you struggle with feeling like you have to work hard to justify your existence on earth, I suggest you read the first book listed in the recommended reading on page 98, *Rethink Your Self* by Trevin Wax. I personally found it very eye-opening. It's one of the reasons why I decided to address this topic of identity in the beginning of this book before jumping into the topic of purposeful branding.

Now just because your identity is not based on your work, it does not give you license to squander the skills, talents, abilities, interests, and passions you've been given. They serve a purpose. Their purpose is to be put to use to meet a need or solve a problem for others. This can be carried out in many ways, roles, and assignments, most frequently through your work and your career.

In other words, there is a difference between your identity, your calling, and your assignment. Here's what this difference looks like:

Identity: Whether you personally believe in a creator or not, all human beings are a reflection of what they came from. This is a commonality all humans share.

Calling: And whether you believe in God or not, you've been given a skill set to be used to better the lives of people from various belief systems. This is what directs your vocation and career and is often referred to as "calling." You'll never be able to do anything you want to do, but you will be able to do what you've been created and equipped to do. In his book *The Call*, Os Guinness says, "Careers that express calling are as fulfilling as careers that contradict calling are frustrating."

Assignment: Your skills are used in various assignments throughout your life and career. For example, your first job was one temporary assignment. The same is true for your current job and your next job. It's also true for any role in which you have a responsibility (i.e., parent, caregiver, etc.).

At one point in my life, my assignment was to be a student. This role of student at times also included the role of intern. Once I graduated, I took on a new assignment as a career coach. Within this role I've also served as a speaker and an author. Throughout these educational and career assignments, I've also had personal assignments and held the roles of friend, sister, daughter, caregiver, wife, and more.

In summary, your identity is found not in what you've created, but in what created you.

Your calling is your overall and ongoing use of the toolbox of skills, talents, abilities, passions, and experiences.

Your assignments are specific opportunities or tasks for specific times when you'll use your toolbox to help others. They are temporary, and you will have many assignments throughout your career and your lifetime.

In your lifetime you have one identity, a handful of skills, and many assignments.

What Makes You Unique?

You have something to contribute to this world because you are here. You're an original, uniquely created to make a difference (big or small) in the world.

But can you answer the question, "What makes you unique?"

Are you comfortable talking about yourself in this way?

Most people aren't. They often say they feel like they're bragging when trying to answer this question. But in certain situations, it's necessary to explain what makes you unique. Those situations can include a job interview or potential promotion, a pitch of your services to potential clients, a presentation to potential investors, and a variety of other scenarios.

For my past recording artist clients, they often had to answer this question when meeting with potential record labels in the hopes of being signed to the label. One client named Claire had to verbally describe what made her music so unique (which it very much was) in addition to just playing her music for the record executives.

I also have to answer this question myself when meeting with potential clients. I know there are many other career coaches they have to choose from. Being able to share what makes me unique from other career coaches gives me freedom from insecurity and discouragement which comes from making unnecessary comparisons. (I'll talk more about what I mean by this later in this chapter.) It also allows me to determine if the potential client and I will be the right fit for each other.

Therefore, talking about your uniqueness isn't about bragging, or even about "selling yourself." It's about accurately telling your audience what you can help them accomplish, and how you do it differently from others who offer the same help, so they can make an informed decision. It's not arrogant to be accurate and honest about what you're good at.

However, one thing to remember as you go through this process is, you're not a unicorn. You're not so unique that you have skills no one else has ever possessed in the history of the world. There are people who may have similar skills and abilities as your own, and may serve the same type of people as you do. But your past assignments, and experiences (good or bad), combined with the creative way you've used your skills, is part of what makes you unique. You're no better and no less than anyone with similar strengths, just different. It's in your different life experiences where your purpose(s) will be used.

In the book *How to Land the Job of Your Dreams*, author Chip Ingram says, "By recognizing your calling and authentic self, you gain the grace to acknowledge others in their calling and their unique set of gifts and abilities."

Yes, bragging is wrong. But the other extreme is just as wrong. Trying too hard to sound like you're not bragging by downplaying your strengths leads to false modesty. Lying about how bad you are at something is no different from lying about how good you are at something.

To find the appropriate balance, you have to be honest with yourself and accurate with others. This is what true authenticity is about. When you take this approach to articulating and communicating your purposeful brand, people will instinctively sense you're being genuine. As a result, they'll want to invest in what you have to contribute to them and your community.

The Purpose of Purposeful Branding

While there are times you have to talk about yourself in order to describe your uniqueness, the goal isn't to *keep* talking about yourself. *The goal is to build trust so others will do the talking and spread the word about how you can help people.*

The purpose of branding is for others to immediately think of your message and then picture in their minds the uniqueness you represent and the message you want to convey, without you saying a word.

For example, let's take a trusted brand most people are familiar with: Mercedes-Benz. When people see the Mercedes logo or hear the Mercedes name, they typically think of two things: luxury and safety.

Mercedes doesn't have to say in their advertisements their cars are luxurious or safe. Everyone already knows it. But in the beginning, they had to educate and inform the public on what makes them different and unique.

So do you!

The Process of Purposeful Branding

In my previous work with up-and-coming recording artists, I taught them how to refine their brand and articulate it to the people who could make or break their careers. This included several key audiences such as their fans, potential record labels, radio stations, potential corporate sponsors, talent buyers, venue owners, and potential team members (i.e., publicists, managers, producers, etc.).

This book will take you through a similar process to help you refine and articulate your own purposeful brand. The focus will be on three key phases:

Phase I – Preparation: identifying your differentiators.

Phase II – Packaging: refining your purposeful branding message.

Phase III – Presentation: articulating and enhancing your purposeful brand.

Within each of these key areas, you'll learn the following:

- How to determine what makes you unique or different. This is the cure for imposter syndrome.
- How your specific gifting can best serve others.
- How to articulate the ways you can serve others.

- How to get to know your particular audience(s) you will serve and genuinely engage with them.
- How to create a vision statement, mission statement, and unique selling point (USP) to help you stay focused.
- What you need to establish authenticity and credibility.

What you'll also learn from this process is how to stop comparing yourself to others as if you are better or worse than them.

I remember presenting on this topic at a program hosted by the Nashville Arts & Business Council. After going through all three phases of this program, one of the participants broke down in tears. She was a young, aspiring singer/songwriter, and up until then had been comparing herself to other singers in town.

This young lady shared how damaging unnecessary comparison had been to her self-esteem. She said her tears were tears of relief because this program helped her to see she doesn't have to compare herself to her competition now that she can better pinpoint her own uniqueness.

When you focus on your audience's needs and how you can use your difference to make a difference in their lives, comparison with your competition becomes a comparison of apples and oranges.

Examining your life and taking stock of your differences and uniqueness can be fun, eye-opening, and scary all at the same time. But the world needs more people who are courageous enough to do so.

Saint Paul said, "Pay careful attention to your own work, for then you will get the satisfaction of a job well done, and you won't need to compare yourself to anyone else." In other words, carefully examine and explore the work you've been given, and devote yourself to it. Don't be impressed with yourself, and don't compare yourself with others. Instead, take responsibility with your own life and work, and do the best you can with your own gifting and strengths.

Congrats on challenging yourself to step out of your comfort zone and into the transparency of your humanity, and for taking an honest look at your strengths and weaknesses.

By the end of this process, you'll have a clearer understanding of how your purpose(s) can best be used in this world and for your community. This will likely result in a healthy level of confidence, increased productivity, career growth, more job satisfaction, less impostor syndrome, and less stress and depression.

Next, we will focus on taking stock of the things that equip you for your purpose(s). This includes your values and your personal and career goals. It also includes both your likes and dislikes, and your strengths and weaknesses.

It's important to not only understand your interests and strengths but also your limitations so you're not wasting your time and energy trying to do something you weren't created to do. You must honor your limits as much as you honor your strengths.

PHASE I – PREPARATION: IDENTIFYING AND DEFINING YOUR PURPOSEFUL BRAND

In Limbo and Feeling Stuck

One definition of the word "trigger" is, "a life event that forces you into limbo." Some people refer to this as "feeling stuck."

Limbo is exactly what I found myself in several years ago.

What was the life event forcing me into limbo? Nothing I would describe as an "event" occurred. But my time of limbo lasted for a good year and a half.

During the summer of 2014, whenever I wasn't busy with my work as an image consultant, I packed in as many fun activities into my schedule as I could: parasailing, stand-up paddleboarding, kayaking, hiking, biking, rock climbing and more. Heck, I even got to ride in a race car during one of the video shoots I was working on. It was absolutely exhilarating!

Looking back, I now realize that getting out and experiencing some things outside of my normal routine and comfort zone was probably my trigger (in a good way).

Why? Because it made me examine myself and re-think some things in my career and my business. This process helped me in so many ways. It made me want to help others who were going through a similar state of limbo and career uncertainty.

But at the time, I couldn't see exactly what this looked like. I started feeling restless and burned out with my image consulting work I once was very passionate about. And I was lacking a vision and purpose for the future of my business which made it feel like a dead end.

Despite having the time to do some fun things, I was definitely in limbo, which is not always a fun place to be.

During my limbo phase, I couldn't figure out what I wanted to do or what was next for me career-wise. It was frustrating and discouraging.

All I know is, during the summer of 2014, people were coming to me with the same struggles. They were suffering from burnout and needed some kind of change in their lives and careers (much like how people felt after the first year of the pandemic). How they wished they could have the courage and means to step out of their comfort zone and discover some new passions and interests like I had.

Every time I heard this my heart would go out to them. I would say, "You CAN!" But my encouragement was always met with some kind of obstacle, either real or perceived.

Their responses included reasons (or are they excuses?) such as, "I don't have the money." Or, "I don't have the time." Or, "I don't have the skill/education," etc., etc., etc.

I think a lot of those examples could easily be translated to "I don't have the courage." This is understandable because fear can be extremely paralyzing, whether it's fear of the unknown, fear of failure, or fear of change.

The summer turned into fall, then winter and then summer again. I continued trying and doing new things to help me make sense of the uncertainty I was experiencing.

I went ice skating for the first time in my life, took a fly-fishing class, and learned archery, just to challenge myself physically and mentally.

During this time, I also continued my favorite activity I had picked up the previous summer, stand-up paddleboarding. I have three boards now and paddleboard in every season, even in the dead of winter, because I am so very passionate about it.

Also, I did something in September 2015 I never imagined doing. I paddled 16.4 miles from downtown Nashville's Nissan Stadium on the winding Cumberland River to Rock Harbor Marina. I thought it would take me about five or six hours to complete. But I finished in a little over four hours, all while going against a headwind with little to no current to help carry me downstream on my board.

Although I couldn't see the finish line because of all the twists and turns in the river, it eventually would become clear as I neared it, even if it took what seemed like forever. All I had to do was be patient and keep moving one paddle stroke at a time.

This is exactly what I did in my time of limbo. I patiently kept doing the little bit I knew to do at a time. This included asking myself a lot of tough questions and examining my answers, along with praying a lot, all while waiting for guidance to come.

Exercise: Self-Examination

Can you relate to feeling stuck or being in limbo? Is this where you are right now?

The first step in getting unstuck is to spend some focused quiet time examining and honestly answering some challenging but helpful questions.

Below is a list of suggested questions. These are some of the same questions I ask my clients when I first begin working with them. Feel free to add questions of your own to this list.

Try to answer as many of these questions as you can. If you can't answer them all, don't worry. You can always come back to some of them after you've completed the other exercises in this book.

Record your answers where you can easily access them again later (space is provided on pages 104-115). Your answers will come in handy as you work through this book.

1. What ways do you enjoy helping others the most?
2. What do you want to be known for, or as? (Hint: think in terms of traits instead of accomplishments.)

3. Do you reflect this in your life?
4. Do you reflect this in your work?
5. What are your long-term and short-term goals? (If you haven't done any goal-setting, you'll want to review the paNASH *8-Step Goal-Achievement Plan* which is available for free when you subscribe to the paNASH newsletter at www.yourpassioninlife.com.)
6. What are two of your interests or passions? (Think not just in terms of hobbies, but also in terms of the skills you enjoy using most, the things you lose track of time while doing, the causes that are important to you, and the things you're willing to suffer or make a sacrifice for.)
7. How can you combine your two interests? This "marriage" of interests could be part of what makes you unique! (Note: most people need help answering this question, which is something I do in coaching my clients. When trying to answer this question on your own, allow yourself to be creative. Don't edit yourself or dismiss any idea that seems silly or impossible. You'd be surprised at how you can come up with something possible

when you take the time to consider the impossible.)

8. What are your differentiating factors: characteristics, traits, and/or experiences you have to offer which set you apart? (We'll delve into this more in another exercise which will help you better answer this question. But for now, start chewing on this question and jot down anything that comes to mind.)
9. What one word best describes you?
10. What are some synonyms of this word?
11. Ask yourself, "Do I reflect this in everything I do? In how I communicate with others, in my work, in my interaction with friends/family/audience, etc.?"
12. Who's your audience? (I.e., if you're a business owner, then your clients, strategic partners, and investors would be your audience; if you're a job seeker, then recruiters, hiring managers, and networking contacts would be your audience; if you want to write a book, then potential readers, publishers, agents, and publicists would be your audience.) Think of as many categories of potential audience members you may have. Don't

worry if you're having a difficult time answering this question right now. We'll flesh it out later in this process.

13. What kind of experience do you want to create for your audience? (Note: this is not about people pleasing. Instead, it's about the kind of experience you want your audience to have as you help them with their needs and deliver your service to them.)
14. What level of transparency are you comfortable with?
15. Most importantly: WHY DO YOU DO WHAT YOU DO? Do not move forward until you can answer this question, even if it's just in a rough draft. A great resource for this question is the TEDTalk "How Great Leaders Inspire Action" by Simon Sinek. It's one of the most viewed talks of all time. It's an oldie but goodie!

To get an idea of how this process works, let's walk through answering question #9, "What one word best describes you?"

This can be a difficult question to answer. Try to think about the first thing that comes to mind. Also, think about what others have said about you in the past.

It doesn't necessarily have to be anything brimming with positivity. Examples can include opinionated, insightful, cynical, optimistic, etc. It can be positive or negative. Or it can be something that could be negative in others' opinions but positive in your own opinion.

Now, write your word down in the middle of a piece of paper and circle it. Next, create a mind map by drawing branches out from your word and write out some synonyms of your word.

While doing this you might find some more positive words for your original word which may have had some unwanted negative connotations.

For instance, I had a client who first described herself as a "rebel." She wasn't very excited about this word but knew it was how she's often perceived. Once she started branching off from the word "rebel," she realized she's more of a change-agent and a catalyst for change. These synonyms made her feel more confident.

Once your mind map is complete, look at it and ask yourself, "Do I reflect this in all I do?" (i.e., in how I communicate with others, even in my status updates on social media, and in how I interact with others).

Hang on to this mind map because we'll use it again later.

Exercise: Take an Inventory

While going through my time of limbo, I also took a personal inventory of the strengths I have to offer to others in my community and in the marketplace.

And I took a hard look at my weaknesses so I could know what I should invest time improving upon and where I shouldn't waste time trying to be something I'm not.

There are two reasons why it's important to know your weaknesses. First, knowing your weaknesses and being able to admit them makes you relatable and empathetic toward others.

Second, it's important to understand your weaknesses so you can avoid saying "yes" to the wrong things and learn how to say "no."

You don't want your brand to be "The 'YES' person." When this happens, you are the one everyone will turn to for everything. You'll be the dumping ground for the things others don't want to do.

I saw this happen with a former supervisor of mine. She would get asked to take on a certain project or head up a committee and she'd always say yes. As a result, she was the one who always received such requests.

Eventually, she was working on projects which had nothing to do with her gifting or her goals and mission, or even her own job description. She quickly got burned out and became resentful.

If you're someone who also has a hard time saying no to things you shouldn't do, the following exercise will be very helpful for you, along with the personal mission statement exercise we'll do later in the book.

To take a personal inventory, make a list of the following items:

- Your past accomplishments.
- Your strengths and skills (and not just your work-related skills).
- The ways your skills benefit others.
- The additional ways your skills benefit others, or the by-products of the help you provide others.
- Your limitations and weaknesses.

- Your biggest failures and their redemptive perspective (meaning, what's something good that came from each of your failures?).
- Your reasons for why you like to do the things you do best.

Exercise: Fieldwork

Once you've completed some or all of the self-examination questions and the inventory, it's time to do some fieldwork.

This is where you find out what qualities other people associate with you and what they already think of when they think of you. It's a way to gauge your current brand, because guess what? You already have a brand whether you realized it or not!

Gauging what others think of you helps you know what you personally would like to improve upon.

But understand, this process should not be used to give other people's opinions control over you. You need to take the feedback as objectively as you can instead of worrying or caring too much about what others think of you. It's designed to build your confidence while also helping you be realistic about your current brand.

Before beginning this exercise, make sure you're in a place where you can receive both positive and negative constructive criticism.

You have to be open to stepping a bit outside your comfort zone to complete this exercise. If you're the type who's easily offended, you may have to give yourself a little extra time with this exercise so you don't immediately react to your initial emotions.

In this exercise you'll send an email to five or more people, including friends, family, co-workers, acquaintances, etc. from your different circles. Ask them to list the things they think of when they think of you.

Emphasize to them they should include both positive AND negative examples.

Tell them not to be shy, but instead to be completely honest. Let them know it's SAFE and necessary for them to share some negative things because you'll use the feedback for constructive purposes.

Remember, before you do this, you must be prepared to be *open and receptive* to the feedback without being offended.

Give your contacts a deadline of about three to five days to get this information back to you. You don't want them to take too much time in providing their responses because you want them to go with the first things that come to mind about you.

Once you receive the responses from your friends, answer the following questions:

Which responses came as a surprise to you? Maybe your contacts used a word you define differently than they do.

For example, others have described me as a leader, but I don't tend to think of myself as a leader. This is because I have an idea in my own head of what a leader is, and I realized it's different from other people's ideas of a leader.

What kind of pattern do you see in the responses? Do some of their descriptions match the synonyms on your mind map?

Hang on to the responses you've collected in this exercise because they'll be helpful in other exercises in this book.

Exercise: Peeling the Onion

I remember when I worked as an image consultant, I met with a potential client who'd just moved from New York to Nashville. He was an aspiring singer/songwriter and was interested in some wardrobe styling services.

I mentioned to him I also provided coaching services to prepare him for meetings with labels and music publishers, which is similar to interview prep. He said he didn't need those services and just wanted the wardrobe styling services.

I told him I understood and went on with our meeting. In order to learn more about him, I asked him what made him different from all the other aspiring artists who've moved to Nashville to pursue music.

He sat straight up, puffed out his chest, and said, "That's easy, my talent!"

I smiled and said, "Welcome to Nashville where *everyone* is talented. What makes *you* different from all the other talented aspiring artists here?"

His chest fell, and his mouth gaped open. He realized he had no answer to this question. This is when he said, "Maybe I do need some of those other services you offer."

It was this conversation which gave birth to the following exercise. I refer to it as "peeling the onion."

Here's how it works:

1. In the following question, insert a word or phrase best describing your uniqueness: "What makes me different from others (i.e., my peers or my competitors) who are also _____?" (Note: you can use your answer to the question, "What one word best describes you?", or a word from your fieldwork responses.)
2. Now answer the above question using some of the other words from your synonyms or the fieldwork responses. For instance, if you said you're unique because you're creative, ask yourself what makes you different from others who are also creative?
3. Keep peeling the onion. For example, if you said you're creative and hard-working, ask yourself what makes you different from others who are also creative and hard-working. Therefore, what makes

you different from others who are _____ and _____?

4. Keep going with this line of questioning to see if you can add two to three more differentiators.

Of course, as I stated in the previous chapter, there will always be people with similar traits and strengths as your own. But, by digging a little deeper, you'll discover things about yourself you hadn't previously considered. It often helps to work one-on-one with a coach on this.

If you're interested in working one-on-one, email me at lorib@yourpassioninlife.com.

Remember, the things you discover about yourself in this process are the essence of your purposeful brand.

Exercise: Know Your Audience

While it's important to understand and know your own differentiators, it's also important to understand the uniqueness of your intended audience, the people you were created to serve. This helps you know how to engage and interact with them, along with how to communicate the ways you can best serve them.

For example, when I was working as an image consultant, one of my clients (a five-person band) really wanted a specific producer for their debut album. But because this producer was well-known, the band knew he had his pick of artists and projects to choose from. And they knew since they were still unheard of, they'd have to convince this producer to take on their project.

As a result, they enlisted my help to prepare their pitch. This included being able to speak to this producer's interests and to articulate WHY he should take them on as a client.

They would never be able to convince him if they couldn't tell him what made them different and how their uniqueness aligned with his own uniqueness.

Just like recording artists have several layers of audiences (i.e., their team of industry professionals they hope to work with, fans, labels, media outlets, sponsors, venues, and talent buyers), you too have a variety of audiences for what you're trying to accomplish.

If you're a job seeker, your audience would likely include hiring managers, recruiters, networking contacts, etc.

If you're currently employed, your audience would likely include your boss, co-workers, subordinates, clients, customers, shareholders, etc.

If you're starting your own business, your audience would likely include current customers and clients, potential customers and clients, investors, strategic partners, vendors, employees, etc.

In your personal life, your audience likely includes your family, friends, neighbors, acquaintances, community, church, etc.

The things you need to research and understand about your audience are:

- Their demographics (age, gender, geographic location).
- What they care about (i.e., are they recruiters looking to hire for specific job positions?).
- Where they spend their time online. What social media platforms do they use the most? What kind of blogs do they read? What kind of podcasts do they listen to? What LinkedIn and Facebook groups do they belong to?

- How they find out about new information and new trends.
- Their favorite hobbies.
- How they can identify something important about themselves in your purposeful brand.
- MOST IMPORTANTLY: the biggest **challenge** your audience faces and how your purposeful brand solves this problem or benefits the audience.

Another thing to consider about your audience is to determine which members fall into which of these four categories:

1. Those who already have the same skills and offerings you have (those who know what they know).
2. Those who know they need your skills but don't possess them themselves (those who know what they don't know).
3. Those who have your same skills but don't know how to use them (those who don't know what they know).
4. Those who don't have your skills and don't think they need your skills (those who don't know what they don't know).

It's the people in categories two and three with whom you should spend your time and energy. These are the people who will get your "why" and will see the value in what you have to offer.

The people in the other two categories won't get it, at least not right away or not until you've developed a strong purposeful brand.

Once you've become knowledgeable about your audience, start to consider at what level you'd be interested in making an impact on your audience. What I mean by this is, do you prefer directly helping individuals, or groups of people?

Or, do you prefer to have a broader impact where you aren't working directly with your audience, but instead you're helping them indirectly by improving policies, systems, or institutions affecting them? Or do you prefer to have a global impact on people?

In addition, consider if you want to impact your audience by creating new ways to help them, fixing broken ways of helping them, or supporting and maintaining currently successful ways of helping them.

Personally, I know I'm most suited for working with people one-on-one. And I enjoy creating new ways for them to develop their career and conduct a job search, while mixing in the tried-and-true strategies which remain timeless.

Next Steps

All the exercises in this first phase (the preparation phase) are designed to provide you the information needed to accomplish the next two phases.

In addition, your responses and answers in the previous exercises can assist you with the job search process. You can pull from your responses keywords to use in your resume, along with answers to possible job interview questions (i.e. "What is your greatest strength/weakness?", "Tell me about a time when…", and more).

Hang on to your work from each exercise you've completed thus far because we'll use it in packaging your purposeful brand in Phase II.

Phase II – Packaging: Creating and Building Your Purposeful Brand

Coming Out of Limbo

After a year and a half of being stuck in limbo, I had a day where I suddenly got a realization of what was next for me in my career.

I realized part of my purpose is to help other people discover and pursue their passions and interests, and help them weave them through their career and personal lives. This also includes helping them find ways over, through, or around the obstacles and fears keeping them from their passions.

As soon as I had this realization, I could clearly see ways of helping people do this, using my own unique strengths and passions, along with the things I've learned from my past professional experience. Immediately after, I received numerous confirmations this was truly my new path.

It's like getting all my thoughts out of my head and onto paper created some much-needed head and heart space for this realization to form. I honestly don't believe this answer would have come to me had I not done the self-examination and other exercises outlined in Phase I.

Now, I'm not saying it will happen like this for you exactly the way it happened for me. But I've seen clients who've spent the time and energy on the exercises in Phase I gain clarity in several areas, including:

- Who they are as a person.
- What they represent.
- What they value most.
- What their purposes are.
- How their strengths and skills line up with their purposes.
- Why the things they were trying before weren't working.
- How to embrace their differences.
- And more!

All of these things have had a positive impact on various aspects of their lives and careers.

While Phase I probably felt like a lot of work, it's very important work, which serves as the biggest piece of the puzzle in determining your uniqueness and how to get your authentic message and purposeful brand across.

Now it's time to take what you did in Phase I and complete Phase II.

What's Your Message?

In Phase I, you determined the following:

1. Who your audience is (the people who'll like the skills and strengths you have to offer).
2. The biggest problem(s) or challenge(s) your audience faces.
3. How you are able to solve your audience's problems with your own set of skills and strengths (what makes you unique).
4. Your #1 strength or benefit you have to offer your audience (which solves their problem).
5. The deeper core benefits for your audience (the additional benefits your skills offer to your audience; your promises to your target market).

The information above is what will help you in formulating your **vision statement, mission statement**, and **Unique Selling Point (USP)** which all serve as your purposeful branding message.

When most people hear the terms "vision statement," "mission statement," and "USP," they think of them as things a company, institution, or organization uses to communicate to their audience what their organization is all about.

But these concepts aren't just for businesses or organizations. They're also important for individuals like you. They help you make important life and career decisions, achieve your goals, and serve others better.

Let's look at what each one is exactly.

Vision Statement

A **vision statement** is simply your answer to your **"Why?"** question. It's *why you do what you do* and it paints a picture of your desired future.

It's your purpose(s). Like the TEDTalk said, people don't buy *what* you do. They buy *why* you do it. They're more interested in your "why" before your "how" or your "what."

This is similar to the popular quote by Theodore Roosevelt, "People don't care how much you know until they know how much you care." Your "why" is what you care about. You do what you do because you care.

My personal vision statement is the same as my vision statement for my company, paNASH. They both state:

"I believe everyone can find the courage to discover and pursue their passions despite the obstacles they may face. I want to see people actively pursue their passions with flair ('paNASH') and confidence, along with responsibility to their purpose in life."

Mission Statement

A lot of so-called experts like to say your mission statement is your "why," but it's simply not the case. If your vision statement is your "why," then your **mission statement** is your "**how**." It explains *how you plan to achieve your vision.*

For example, paNASH's mission statement is:

"To serve, educate, and encourage others by assisting them with the discovery and pursuit of their passions in a way that honors their purpose and their own vision for success, while amplifying who they are personally and advancing them professionally."

My personal mission statement is:

"To boldly pursue my passions and purpose, and to teach, encourage, and inspire others to do the same, resulting in lives overflowing with joy, peace, and fulfillment."

This personal mission statement is broad enough for me to carry it out in both my work and in other areas of my life.

I use my mission statements to help me make important life and business decisions. I compare my options to the appropriate mission statement, and if they don't support my mission statement, I don't choose them. This saves me from spending time and energy on things I shouldn't be doing.

For example, at the time I first wrote my personal mission statement in late 2015, my friendship with my guy-friend was turning romantic. The relationship was great at first. But, after nine months of dating, I noticed a pattern had been developing for some time. This pattern wouldn't make such a relationship sustainable if certain variables remained the same, which they did.

I wasn't sure if I should end the relationship or give it another chance. After much prayer, I was reminded of my mission statement and why I'd written it. So, I pulled it out and started reading it. I immediately realized the relationship didn't support the life goals in my mission statement.

Though I didn't want to end the relationship, I had to before we were committed in marriage so I could stay true to my God-given purpose. It wasn't an easy thing to do because my heart didn't feel like ending it. But my soul knew what was best for me in the long run.

I had to be disciplined enough to push through my fickle emotions which were temporary, and focus on the decision that would make me happier and healthier down the road.

Once I ended the relationship, I received confirmation in so many forms (including red flags I previously didn't notice) and realized I had indeed made the right decision. Anytime I considered turning back, those red flags served as reminders as to why I had to stick to my decision. Luckily, he and I were able to become friends again, so the friendship wasn't lost. I'm now married to a wonderful man who shares similar values and goals with me.

I also use the paNASH mission statement when making tough decisions in my business.

There are so many ways a mission statement can help you in making various decisions.

It can help you say no to something you shouldn't say yes to. All you have to do is compare the decision at hand with your mission statement and ask yourself if it supports your mission statement (while also considering other factors involved when necessary). If it doesn't, then likely you can say no.

It can also help you advance in your career. For example, a mission statement serves as a basis for an answer to the interview question, "Can you tell us about yourself?" (I share how to answer this interview question in the on-demand program entitled *Steps to Acing the Interview and Reducing Your Interview Anxiety*.)

Go to www.yourpassioninlife.com/ondemand for more info on the program *Steps to Acing the Interview and Reducing Your Interview Anxiety*.

I've seen clients tailor their mission statement for their answer to this interview question and land the job.

I even had a client get promoted because of her mission statement. She was on a conference call with her co-workers and the Vice President of the company. The VP asked if anyone on the call had a mission statement.

She was the only one who did and was asked to share it. The VP was so impressed with her mission statement he insisted she be promoted in her department!

USP

A **USP** (Unique Selling Point) is "**what**" distinguishes you, your business, or your craft from others offering the same skills, services, or products. (Some people call it a "unique selling proposition," and either phrase works for our purposes here.)

paNASH's USP is:

"Helping you get unstuck so you can put your passion into action!"

I purposely chose to use the word "unstuck" because it's the same language my audience uses when approaching me for help and self-describing their own challenges.

Once you get to know your own audience better, you'll start to pick up on some patterns they use to describe their challenges. Always use the same language you hear over and over from your audience to tweak your message so it will resonate with those you're trying to reach.

Your USP can be fun, attention-grabbing, or even humorous. Remember Claire, the recording artist who had a very unique sound to her music? Her USP is "I make music for people who are bad at dancing." Pretty funny and clever!

You want your message to be short and concise enough to fit in a tweet so it's easy for you and others to remember. It's best to stick to 25 words or less for a USP.

Please note: a USP is not the same thing as an elevator pitch (to learn the difference and how to create your own elevator pitch, go to www.yourpassioninlife.com/blog and search "elevator speech"). Instead, it's best used in your social media platforms such as in your LinkedIn headline or your Instagram bio, in your email signature, or on your business card.

Exercise: Drafting Your Message

Now that you understand the difference between a vision statement, mission statement, and USP, it's time to start writing your own message. There's no one right way to do this, but I've provided some suggestions below to assist you in the process. Feel free to use them or your own method.

Just remember, be yourself!

Your message should tell people who you are and what you stand for, not what you do (because what you do may change several times in your career). So avoid any industry-specific jargon from your work life.

Don't be afraid to be transparent or vulnerable. And don't worry about what others will think!

Writing a Vision Statement

In thinking about what you want your vision statement to say, consider your dreams, your desired future (at least one to five years from now), and your personal definition of success.

Write your vision statement in the present tense. Infuse it with passion and purpose, and paint a visual picture of it with your words.

_____
_____
_____
_____
_____

Writing a Mission Statement

If you need help with writing your mission statement, you can start with the following simple formula, using the information you collected from Phase I.

Formula:

Step one, consider your previous answers to the following five questions:

1. Who is your audience/target market (the people who'll like the skills and strengths you have to offer)?
2. What's the biggest problem(s) or challenge(s) your audience faces?
3. How are you able to solve your audience's problems with your skills and strengths (what makes you unique)?
4. What's your #1 strength or benefit you have to offer your audience which solves their problem?
5. What are the deeper core benefits for your market (the additional benefits your skills offer to your audience; your promises to your target market)?

Step two, insert your answers matching up with the questions in the appropriate brackets:

- Short version of your message: "I help [Q1] [Q5]."
- Medium version of your message: "I help [Q1]. You know how [Q1] [Q2]? Well, what I do is [Q3] and [Q5]."
- Long version of your message: "I help [Q1] solve [Q2] by [Q3] resulting in [Q4] and [Q5]."

You don't have to follow this formula exactly as it's laid out. You can be flexible and word it in whatever way makes the most sense for you.

_____
_____
_____
_____
_____
_____
_____

Writing a USP

Your USP can either be the short version of your mission statement, or something similar showing your unique approach to solving your audience's biggest challenges. Write your USP keeping it short and simple:

_____

_____

_____

_____

Remember, your vision statement, mission statement, and USP are ways to articulate your purposeful brand to those who are still learning what you're about.

You'll want to have them consistently posted in appropriate places. For instance, your USP can be on your business card and in the headline of your LinkedIn profile. Your vision and mission statements can be in the "About" section of your LinkedIn profile and on your web site.

Can you think of some other places you can post your statements? How about your Instagram bio? Where else can you display your statements?

The more you consistently put your message out there, the more your name will become synonymous with your message.

Don't Forget About Your Goals

It's important to note, your short-term and long-term goals should be in direct support of your vision and mission statements. Any goals not supporting your vision and mission statements should either be redirected or put on hold for now.

If you need help with setting and achieving your goals, I suggest you review the free download of the *8-Step Goal-Achievement Plan* you received when you subscribed to the paNASH newsletter at www.yourpassioninlife.com.

Back It Up

To show authenticity and credibility, you should be able to back up everything you've said in your vision statement, mission statement, and USP.

This is done through a variety of items you can include in your purposeful branding package, depending on your goals, industry, situation, etc.:

- Resume or CV
- Bio
- LinkedIn profile
- Letters of reference, recommendations, or testimonials
- Press kit
- Professional portfolio (samples of your past work)
- Personal or professional blog

- Certifications
- A list of skills you've gained outside your professional life (i.e., from volunteer activities, sports, hobbies, interests, recreation, travel, passion projects, side hustles, continuing education classes, etc.)
- Anything you can think of providing credibility to your purposeful brand and your message

Note: Both one-on-one coaching and on-demand videos are available to assist you with the development of your resume, LinkedIn profile, and professional portfolio. Email me at lorib@yourpassioninlife.com for more info.

Additional Packaging Steps

Other ways to package your brand and back it up include:

- <u>Staying current</u>: Remain well-read and stay abreast of your area of expertise, knowledge, or interest.
- <u>Creating connections</u>: Create key connections and strategic partnerships with people you admire and those providing complimentary services. You accomplish this through networking. (To learn how to network naturally and effectively, check out

paNASH's on-demand program on networking at www.yourpassioninlife.com/ondemand.)

- <u>Sharing your expertise</u>: Provide thoughtful comments and responses to social media posts on your area of expertise. This helps get your name out there to your audience.

Before we move on to the third and final phase of the purposeful branding process, I want to point out there can be some overlap between Phase II, the packaging phase, and Phase III, the presentation phase. This doesn't change the effectiveness of the process.

Now let's explore this final phase to see how it all comes together.

Phase III – Presentation: Articulating and Enhancing Your Purposeful Brand

Building Confidence

You've now done the hard work in Phases I and II. Now it's time to put it all together in Phase III.

This phase is all about learning how to present your purposeful brand effectively and with confidence to your intended audience.

To do this, you must:

Exhibit strong communication skills, especially active listening skills.

It's always important to listen to your audience so you can put yourself in their shoes to better understand *their* needs, challenges, feelings, and pain points to see how those perspectives may shift.

Paying attention to those shifts and having important conversations where you're talking less about yourself and more about your different audiences' needs will help you to know just how your purposeful brand works and who it works for.

For example, when I conduct complimentary initial consultations with potential clients, I spend the majority of my time asking them questions about their specific situation. Then, I spend time listening to their answers and asking follow-up questions. It's only after this do I begin to talk about my services.

Maintain good interpersonal skills ("people" skills).

Relationship building is at the forefront of networking and will help you develop strategic partnerships and grow your audience. Always maintain a give-and-take approach. Be willing to help those who help you. (See Appendix for additional information.)

Clearly articulate your purposeful brand and your added value (i.e., your unique differentiators).

Now that you've discovered your unique differentiators and written out your messages (vision statement, mission statement, and USP), you have a way to articulate your "why," your strengths, and how they can help others.

Be concise.

When presenting your message, always try to be concise when you can. Those who want to know more about what you have to offer will become curious and will ask for more information. (See my post about how to write an effective elevator pitch – search "elevator speech" at www.yourpassioninlife.com/blog.)

Practice the delivery of your message.

Practice the delivery of the message you created in Phase II aloud, over and over, until it becomes natural. You can do this by practicing in front of the mirror, with a friend or family member, or any way that works best for you.

Don't worry about trying to memorize it word-for-word. This won't work in normal conversation and not even in an interview or presentation. Instead, try to remember the main points of your message and state them as clearly and concisely as possible.

Pay attention to the reaction you get when weaving your message into regular conversation. If you're piquing people's interest, it's working. If you're not, then you may have to go back and re-write it.

Be your own advocate.

Know when to reach out to your key contacts for support. Never be afraid to ask for help.

Practice proper professional etiquette.

If you're not familiar with professional etiquette, read up on it! There's a big difference between business etiquette and other types of etiquette.

One very specific example of proper etiquette that comes to mind, especially when it comes to networking, is to never use the phrase "Can I pick your brain?" when wanting to learn from someone else. (To understand why, check out the blog post on this topic in the Appendix.)

You can also read more topics about career etiquette on my blog when you access the "career etiquette" category at www.yourpassioninlife.com/blog.

Think big picture.

Be proactive and strategic with your efforts to be visible. This means not posting on every single online platform or showing up to every single networking event. Instead, choose the ones where your audience spends their time (do you remember this from Phase I?).

Use the same language and verbiage they use when you're discussing your unique differentiators.

Be consistent.

The more consistent you are in all of the above, the more people begin to recognize your purposeful brand and know what to expect from you. Once this happens, they start sharing your message with their friends and telling their friends about you.

This word-of-mouth approach can lead to the type of opportunities you're seeking to help you fulfill your purpose(s). It's at this point you don't have to "shout" what you're about. Instead, people will automatically think of those things when they think of you.

Things to Remember

When presenting your purposeful brand, use the above suggestions to help you not worry about what others might think and to keep you from "playing it safe." This is how you OWN YOUR BRAND!

Don't worry about making mistakes, and don't hide your purposeful brand because it's how you attract the right people to serve. The right people are the ones who don't care how much money you make or what your job title is.

The right people are the ones who will remember the sort of person you are and how you were able to help them. Make your purposeful brand more about them than yourself (hence the need to address your audience's biggest challenges), and you'll be blessed with the right audience and the right opportunities!

Conclusion

By following the advice in the three phases I've covered in this book, and in the blog posts listed in the Appendix, you'll become better at talking about yourself without it sounding like you're bragging. You'll be able to educate others about your purposeful brand and how you can best serve them.

This will be helpful in numerous situations, including when networking, interviewing for a job or job promotion, securing investors and clients for your own business, reaching donors for your fundraising efforts, pursuing your personal endeavors, etc.

If you'd like personalized assistance in developing your purposeful brand or in improving your job search and career strategies like networking, resume writing, and interviewing, you can email me directly at the address listed on page 102.

APPENDIX

Recommended Blog Posts

The following blog posts can all be found at www.yourpassioninlife.com/blog. Type the title or a keyword from the title into the search bar, and press enter. Or tap on the link below in the e-book version.

- "'Follow Your Heart' is Bad Advice. REALLY Bad Advice!"
- "The Best Way to Write a Successful Elevator Pitch"
- "How to Be Realistic About Networking"
- "How to Write a Resume: Make it About THEM, Not You"
- "How to Avoid an Epic Fail When Networking"
- "Why 'Can I Pick Your Brain?' Is the Wrong Approach"
- "Do You Want to Take the Work Out of Networking? Here's How"

To read my latest blog posts, go to www.yourpassioninlife.com/spotlight or sign up for blog post alerts at www.yourpassioninlife.com/blog. You'll find topics on **career etiquette**, **out-of-the-box career advice**, and **post-COVID job search advice**. You can also subscribe to the paNASH newsletter at www.yourpassioninlife.com and receive a free copy of the *8-Step Goal-Achievement Plan.*

Recommended Books

- *Rethink Yourself: The Power of Looking Up Before Looking In*, by Trevin Wax
- *The Call: Finding and Fulfilling the Central Purpose of Your Life*, by Os Guinness
- *How to Land the Job of Your Dreams*, by Chip Ingram
- *Every Good Endeavor: Connecting Your Work to God's Work*, by Tim Keller
- *Designing Your Life: How to Build a Well-Lived, Joyful Life*, by Bill Burnette and Dave Evans
- *Designing Your New Work Life: How to Thrive and Change and Find Happiness – and a New Freedom – At Work*, by Bill Burnette and Dave Evans
- *Body of Work: Finding the Thread That Ties Your Story Together*, by Pamela Slim
- *Do Over: Make Today the First Day of Your New Career*, by Jon Acuff
- *The Rhythm of Life: Living Every Day With Passion and Purpose*, by Matthew Kelly

- *I Could Do Anything If I Only Knew What It Was: How to Discover What You Really Want and How to Get It*, by Barbara Sher
- *Don't Waste Your Life*, by John Piper

More books by Lori, available on Amazon

- *Create Your Dream Job*
- *Get Your Resume Read!*
- *Secrets to Networking With Ease*
- *Foolproof Strategies for Acing the Interview and Reducing Interview Anxiety*

Video Courses by Lori

I have created several video courses and downloadable handouts you can access on-demand any time and at any point in your job search to assist you with your most immediate needs. These courses include much of the same valuable information and resources I share with my clients.

Topics include advice and tips on **networking**, **resumes**, **interviewing**, and much more.

Courses range in price from free to affordable. Save when you purchase the course bundle. For more information, go to www.yourpassioninlife.com/ondemand.

paNASH

Contact Information

I encourage you to revisit the exercises in this book about once a year, or at least every time you experience a major life or career change.

If you need assistance, paNASH has several resources on the topics of career development in a variety of formats including:

- one-on-one coaching
- online video courses available on-demand
- free blog posts and articles
- books and e-books

I invite you to check out paNASH's services at www.yourpassioninlife.com to find out how paNASH can help you.

I also invite you to follow @paNASHcoaching on Facebook and Instagram.

You can also reach me directly via email at lorib@yourpassioninlife.com.

Lori Bumgarner Béen, M.Ed.

paNASH: Helping you get unstuck by showing you how to put your passion into action!

ABOUT THE AUTHOR

Lori Bumgarner Béen is the owner of paNASH, a career coaching service that has been ranked as one of the top coaching services in Nashville every consecutive year since 2017. Lori is a certified transformational coach and certified leadership guide with 25 years of career coaching experience, gained from working in universities such as Vanderbilt and Belmont, as well as in private practice.

Lori is also the author of several books, including the Amazon #1 bestselling book *Advance Your Image*. Her work has been published in *The Huffington Post*, *The Daily Positive*, *Thrive Global*, and *INC.*, and she has been featured in *The Wall Street Journal*.

Lori holds a master's degree in education and a bachelor's degree in psychology. Her passions include stand-up paddleboarding, enjoying the outdoors, life-long learning, and encouraging others.

NOTES

Notes

NOTES

Notes

Notes

Notes

Notes

NOTES

Notes

NOTES

Notes

Notes

www.ingramcontent.com/pod-product-compliance
Lightning Source LLC
Chambersburg PA
CBHW050112230526
45470CB00004B/1788